رۆژێک له رۆژان بێ بارانی و ووشکی یهکی زۆر ناوچهیهکی
داگرت بوو که"تههلهت"ی پێ دهگوترا ، مێش و مهگهز به سهر
خهڵکی و مهڕو ماڵاتدا ووروژابوون ، گهرما به تهواوی خهڵکی
بێزار کردبوو .
دزهکه کراسێکی درێژی لهبهر کرد و کلاوێنکی لهسهر نا ، پاش
پیلان دانان چووه ناو بازارهکهوهو به دهنگێنکی بهرز به خهڵکی
گووت :.
ئهگهر ئێوه کووپهڵهیهک زێڕم بدهنێ ئهوهندهی سهرم گهوره بێت ،
من لهگهڵ خواکاندا دهدوێم و داوای بارانیان لێ دهکهم .

One day there was a terrible drought at a place called
Ahlat.

Flies swarmed around the people and the cattle. The heat
almost drove them mad.

The thief put on a long robe and a big turban.

He strode into the market place and declared in a loud
voice,"If you give me a heap of gold as big as my head, I
will speak to the gods and ask them for rain."

هەروەک پێشینان دەڵێن :
" هەرچەنده زمان ئێسکی نی یه بەڵام ئێسک دەشکێنێ " هەروەها
خەڵکیش لەبەر ئەوەی هیچ چارەسەری تریان نەبوو ناچار ڕازی
بوون .
جادووگەرەکە لە ناوەڕاستی بازارەکەدا وەستا ، دەستی بەرەو
ئاسمان بەرز کردەوە و نووسراوی سەر بەردەکەی خوێندەوە .
لەو ئێواره زووەدا پاش چەند ساتێک دنیا تاریک داهات و چەند
دڵۆپه بارانێک بارین ، ئینجا بەدوایدا بارانێکی بەخوڕ دایکرد .

As the saying goes, "Although the tongue has no bones, it
breaks many bones." And the people had no choice other
than to agree.

The Shaman stood in the middle of the market place,
spread out his arms, and called out the spell.

After a few seconds, although it was still the middle of the
afternoon, it grew dark. At first there were a few
raindrops, then the rain came down like a waterfall from
the sky.

خەڵکی لەخۆشیدا هاواریان لێ هەستا ، کوپەڵە زێڕێنکیان بە
جادووکەرەکە بەخشی کە لە سەری گەورەتر بوو .

ڕۆژی دوایی باران خۆشی نەکرد ، ڕۆژی دواتر و دواتریش هەر
بەردەوام بوو .
وای لێ هات لەوەدەچوو کە بارانەکە هەرگیز خۆش نەکات .

Everybody cheered and cheered, and they gave the
Shaman a bag of gold even bigger than his head.

The next day however, it was still raining, and it rained the
following day and the one after that.

It began to look as if the rain was never going to stop.

بارانەکە خەڵکەکەی تەواو سەغڵەت وماندوو کردبوو کێڵگەکانیان
ەک پارچە بووبوو بەقوڕ ، مالەکانیشیان وا تەڕ بووبوو کە
هەیاندەتوانی لەناویدا بژین . چوونەوە بۆ لای جادووکەرەکە تا
اوای لێ بکەن بارانەکە بوەستێنێ .
هەڵام ئەو تەنها جادووی باران بارینی دەزانی ، بەردەکە جادووی
باران وەستانی لەسەر نەنوسرابوو .
جادووکەرەکە بەهەموو شێوەیەک نوسراوی سەر بەردەکەی خوێندەوە
، لە خوارەوە بۆ سەرەوە ، لە چەپەوە بۆ ڕاست و تەنانەت لەسەر
سەری وەستاو خوێندیەوە .

The people grew sick and tired of the rain.

Their fields were turned to mud and their houses were so
wet that they could not live in them any longer.

They went back to the Shaman and asked him to make it
stop raining.

But he only knew how to *make* it rain.

Nothing on the stone told him how to stop it.

He tried saying the magic words backwards, then
sideways; he even tried saying them standing on his head.

بەڵام دیار بوو بێ سوود بوو بارانەکە خۆشی نەدەکرد
لە کۆتاییدا خەڵکەکە ئەوەندە توورە بوویبوون جادووکەرەکەیان
هەڵگرت و بردیان فڕێیان دایه ناو ڕوبارەکەوه .
هەر کە جادووکەرەکە کەوتە ناو ڕوبارەکەوه ، یەکسەر بارانەکە
وەستا .
جادووکەرەکە لافاو بردی و جارێکی تر کەس چاوی بەچارەی
نەکەوتەوە .

Nothing made the rain stop.

At last, the people were so angry that they seized hold of
the Shaman, carried him to the river and threw him in.

No sooner had he struck the water than the rain stopped.

The Shaman, however, was carried away by the flood, and
he was never seen again.

Information about Kurdistan

The old Kurdish saying, "The Kurds have no friends but the mountains" has proved all too true over the years. For although there are 25 million Kurds and they are among the largest ethnic groups in the world, as Sheri Laizer (1991) says there are no sign posts pointing to Kurdistan.

The region in which they live was carved up between Turkey, Iraq, Iran and Syria after the First World War. Consequently, they have for many years been at the mercy of their powerful and often hostile neighbours.

The Kurds response to this situation, their last and strongest weapon, is their sense of identity, their language, traditions, culture, and very importantly, their

Laizer, S. (1991)
Into Kurdistan, Frontiers Under Fire.
Zed Books.(ISBN 0 86232 899 3)

© Hackney PACT

All rights reserved. No part of this publication may be reproduced, stored in a retrieval system, or transmitted in any form or by any means without the prior permission of the publishers.

ISBN 1 873928 10 6

First published by Hackney PACT, March 1993
Design & Production : Learning by Design,
Tower Hamlets PDC, English St., London E3 4TA
Tel. 081 983 1944 Fax 081 983 1932
Copies of this book may be ordered from the above address
at a price of £3.99 plus £0.60p postage each.